Front cover: ***The Ninth of November, 1887-90****; oil on canvas (detail) by William Logsdail (1859-1944). The artist was inspired by the contrast he witnessed at the Lord Mayor's Show between the glittering coach, with its six horses in crimson harness, its coachman, postillion and footmen liveried in gold, and the 'gloom and grime' of London, with the 'drab crowds' huddled along the footway.*
GUILDHALL ART GALLERY, CORPORATION OF LONDON

Photographs. © The Museum of London. In 1982, the Museum of London was commissioned by the Master of the Pageant at Guildhall, John Reid, to undertake comprehensive photographic coverage of Lord Mayor's Day. As a result, the Museum is now the repository of an extensive collection of photographs commemorating the event and administered on behalf of the Lord Mayor.

Lord Mayor's Procession, *1614-15; watercolour and bodycolour, anon. The 'alba amicorum' kept as autograph books by students (particularly those from German protestant universities) on their travels frequently contained illustrations of typical sights and the dress worn in particular localities. Views of state and civic pageantry in London are often recorded, such as this depiction of the Lord Mayor's procession to be seen on Sundays and holidays. It comes from the album of Michael van Meer of Hamburg who was in England in 1614-15.*
EDINBURGH UNIVERSITY LIBRARY

1990
The Museum of London is funded jointly by the Office of Arts & Libraries and the Corporation of the City of London.

Text by Celina Fox
Edited by Caroline Williamson
Photography by Barrington Gray
Designed by Nichola Nixon
Printed by Balding & Mansell, Wisbech
ISBN 0 904818 27 6

TH

'Wl
the
the
upo
the
part, . . . I was so closely imprisoned between the Bums and Bellies of the Multitude, that I was almost squeez'd as flat as a Napkin in a Press.'

The sensations Ned Ward experienced during the Lord Mayor's Show of 1706 would strike a chord with spectators watching the same event through the centuries to the present day.

The mayoralty of London came into existence between 1191 and 1196 during the absence on crusade of the king, Richard the Lionheart. By the early thirteenth century, it was established as annual practice that the newly appointed officer should be presented to the monarch or his justices, who sat at the Palace of Westminster, to swear fealty to him. The journey from the City to Westminster necessitated a procession in state of the Lord Mayor elect, the Aldermen, the Recorder, Sheriffs and other officers. Undertaken on horseback until the 1420s and thereafter by water until 1857, this procession provided the germ of the Lord Mayor's Show.

Processions and their associated pageants had their origin in folk custom, modified by the Church into feast-day celebrations, notably in London at Midsummer on the feast days of St John the Baptist (24 June) and SS Peter and Paul (29 June). The craft guilds, from among whose number the Lord Mayor was chosen, acted as organising intermediaries, for municipal government was in their hands and they alone had the financial resources to fund such occasions. However, the Lord Mayor's Show did not emerge as a separate event until the mid-sixteenth century following the Reformation, when it supplanted the Midsummer Show.

1 (left) ***The Fishmongers' Pageant on Lord Mayor's Day, 1616****; pen and ink and wash with gilding, anon. The pageant, devised to inaugurate the mayoralty of Sir John Lehman of the Fishmongers' Company, was entitled 'Chrysanaleia, or the Golden Fishing'. It was led by an amphibious 'Fishing Busse'.*
THE WORSHIPFUL COMPANY OF FISHMONGERS

By the Jacobean period, it had become highly elaborate, as is shown in a series of anonymous drawings made of the pageant devised by Anthony Munday, for Lord Mayor's Day in 1616 *(1)*. That year the Lord Mayor, John Leman, came from the Fishmongers' Company, so the motifs included his personal crest (the lemon tree), boats, crowned dolphin, mermaids and mermen, and Sir William Walworth (the Lord Mayor from the Fishmongers' Company who was responsible for slaying Wat Tyler in 1381), as well as a pageant devoted to the King of the Moors, which was probably left over from the Goldsmiths' Company procession the previous year.

Occasions for popular celebration were not encouraged during the Interregnum, but after the Restoration Lord Mayor's Day took on a new lease of life. A painting by an unknown Dutch artist working in England depicts the flotilla of livery company barges being rowed to Westminster on a breezy Lord Mayor's Day in 1683, with Banqueting House and Whitehall in the distance. The

2 *(right to left)* ***The New and Late Lord Mayor Proceeding through the City****; The Sword Bearer; Bearers Carrying the Standard of the Salters' Company; and Musicians, 1670s. Black lead and brown wash, by Marcellus Lauron (c.1648-1701).*

PEPYSIAN LIBRARY, MAGDALENE COLLEGE, CAMBRIDGE

émigré artist Marcellus Lauron (1648?-1701) seems to have attended the Show in the City several times in the late 1670s. He drew the Lord Mayor going by barge to Westminster, and having disembarked on his return journey at Blackfriars Stairs, proceeding on horseback in the cavalcade through the City to the Guildhall Banquet, with his sword bearer, standard bearers and musicians *(2)*. A particularly rare survival is the anonymous fan design which depicts the Lord Mayor's Pageant of 1686 at the moment when the chariot of the Virgin Queen of the Mercers' Company is drawn through the old Stocks Market (site of the present-day Mansion House) *(3)*.

3 ***The Chariot of the Virgin Queen, Lord Mayor's Day, 1686****; pen and ink and wash, anon. The Lord Mayor, Sir John Peake (a member of the Mercers' Company whose emblem was the Virgin Queen) is carried in an 'Imperial Chariot of Roman Form', followed by savages or wild men who kept off the crowd.*

THE MUSEUM OF LONDON

4 ***Westminster Bridge from the North on Lord Mayor's Day, 1746****; oil on canvas, by Giovanni Antonio Canal (Canaletto) (1697-1768). Canaletto painted a number of views of the Thames which include the Lord Mayor's Barge, possibly as a method of attracting City patronage. But the scene must also have reminded him of the regattas and festivals of his native Venice. This work commemorates 29 October 1746 when the Lord Mayor, William Benn, accompanied by the Aldermen and other City dignitaries, was rowed upstream to Westminster. His Barge is shown broadside on, preparing to negotiate the new bridge at Westminster, which was nearing completion. Significantly, two Commissioners of the Bridge, the Dukes of Richmond and Bedford, were already patrons of the artist.*

YALE CENTER FOR BRITISH ART, PAUL MELLON COLLECTION

5 *(facing page, above)* ***The Industrious 'Prentice Lord Mayor of London, 1747****; engraving by William Hogarth (1697-1764). Francis Goodchild travels to the Lord Mayor's Banquet, accompanied by the Marshal of the City with his distinctive hat and sword. The east end of St Paul's and Paternoster Row are visible in the background. The City militia (leaning on the post, left) is in no state to contain the disorderly mob.*

THE MUSEUM OF LONDON

By the late seventeenth century, much of the solemn rhetoric and elaborate symbolism of the pageants had lost their meaning for the audience. Samuel Pepys was not over-impressed on the first Lord Mayor's Day following the Restoration by the pageants he watched on Cheapside, 'which were many, and I believe good, for such kind of things, but in themselves poor and absurd'. Specially conceived pageants for the procession were abandoned in 1702, but Lord Mayor's Day was still an excuse for celebration on land and water *(4)*. According to César de Saussure, writing in the 1720s:

'The populace [on Lord Mayor's Day] is particularly insolent and rowdy, turning into lawless freedom the great liberty it enjoys. At these times it is almost dangerous for an honest man and more particularly for a foreigner, if at all well dressed, to walk in the streets, for he runs the great risk of being insulted by the vulgar populace, which is the most cursed brood in existence.'

Such a view is reflected in Hogarth's print, 'The Industrious Prentice Lord-Mayor of London', from Hogarth's moralising cycle *Industry and Idleness*, published in 1747 *(5)*: watched by Frederick Prince of Wales and Princess Augusta, the mob almost overwhelms the hired carriage which since 1711 had been used to transport the new Lord Mayor from the point of disembarkation to the Guildhall. John June's print of 1761 *(6)* depicts for the first time the custom-built Lord Mayor's Coach, surrounded by the crowds who on this occasion were to break out into open rioting. This glittering Rococo

6 *John June (fl.1740-70),* ***A View of Cheapside, as it Appeard on Lord Mayor's Day Last, 1761****; engraving by John June (fl.1740-70). When George III came in the first year of his reign to dine with the new mayor, Sir Samuel Fludyer, Lord Mayor's Day was turned into a political occasion by William Pitt and Lord Temple, who hogged all the honours, and riots ensued.*
THE TRUSTEES OF THE BRITISH MUSEUM

7 ***St Paul's Cathedral with a Civic Procession, 1837****; oil on canvas by David Roberts (1796-1864). Roberts completed two companion paintings of the Lord Mayor's Coach in 1837, the year of Queen Victoria's accession to the throne. In this work, the Coach traverses the west front of St Paul's, with the legendary giants Gog and Magog – paraded in City pageants since at least the fifteenth century – leading the procession behind.*
GUILDHALL ART GALLERY, CORPORATION OF LONDON

8 *(facing page, above)* ***Lord Mayor's Day, 1835****; wood engraving, after George Cruikshank (1792-1878). This caricature envisages the downfall of the City's power and privileges in the wake of the Municipal Reform Act of 1835, with the Mansion House, the Lord Mayor's Coach, and even Gog and Magog up for sale.*
GUILDHALL LIBRARY, CORPORATION OF LONDON

coach provided the centrepiece for many paintings, prints and drawings throughout the nineteenth century, and not only as part of the procession on Lord Mayor's Day. It was used to convey the Lord Mayor on all official occasions *(7)* and thus appears in prints of his annual visit to Christ's Hospital School, royal visitations to the City or state funerals at St Paul's such as that of the Duke of Wellington in 1852.

But something of the lustre of Lord Mayor's Day was lost as competition grew from so many other forms of public spectacle *(8)*. The Lord Mayor ceased to be transported by water to Westminster in 1857, and from 1883 onwards only had to travel as far as the new Law Courts in the Strand to swear his oath of loyalty to the monarch. Following the establishment of the London County Council in 1888, reform to the whole system of City government seemed imminent.

Instead, however, the ancient traditions and pageants associated with the ancient Corporation were revived in a successful bid to boost its importance. In his painting of the Lord Mayor's Procession of 1889 entitled *The Ninth of November (9)*, William Logsdail (1859-1944) conveys from a privileged position at the front of the crowd all the dignity and ceremony of the event. And for the first time, one of the basic attractions of these occasions is honestly rendered: the contrast between the gilded coach with its brilliant entourage, and the grey dampness of a typical London November day.

9 ***The Ninth of November, 1887-90****; oil on canvas by William Logsdail. In contrast to Cruikshank, Logsdail celebrates the triumph of City traditions, despite the threat posed by the establishment of London County Council in 1888. The artist went to enormous pains to achieve authenticity. He was given permission to visit the mayoral stables in Fore Street, while the coachman and footmen went in their liveries to his studio in Primrose Hill to model for him.*
GUILDHALL ART GALLERY, CORPORATION OF LONDON

THE LORD MAYOR'S COACH

The Lord Mayor's Coach is a masterpiece of Rococo craftsmanship, a tribute to the skill and artistry, the luxury production and consumption found in eighteenth-century London. It was formally commissioned on 4 April 1757 and was ready in time for the Lord Mayor's Procession the same year.

The design of coaches, like the design of furniture, was accepted as being part of an architect's sphere of competence in the eighteenth century. The state coach of William III was designed by the Huguenot architect Daniel Marot (1663-1752) in 1698 and built in the Hague; it still survives, having been bought by the Speaker of the House of Commons in the early nineteenth century and used by his successors ever since. Sir William Chambers (1723-96) was selected to design the new royal state coach in 1760. It was first used by George III at the opening of Parliament in 1762 and is famed today as the Coronation Coach.

The Lord Mayor's Coach was designed by Sir Robert Taylor (1714-88) upon the initiative of his patron, the Lord Mayor elect Sir Charles Asgill (d. 1788). Asgill, through his own industry and a fortunate marriage, had risen from being an outdoor collecting clerk at the Lombard Street Bank. In the mid-1750s he commissioned Taylor to design a banking house at 70 Lombard Street, and in the early 1760s Taylor also designed Asgill House, the banker's villa at Richmond. The work of constructing the 'New Grand State Coach' was taken on by Joseph Berry of Leather Lane, Holborn, Master of the Coach-makers' Company in 1749, for a fixed price of £860.

Coach-makers were responsible for overseeing and co-ordinating the work of many other craftsmen *(10-19)*. According to Campbell's *The London Tradesmen* (1747):

'The Coach-Maker's proper Business is to make the Body of the Coach, and all the Carriage except the Wheels; his trade is compounded of the Carpenter, Taylor, and

10 *The coachmaker was required to furnish the inside of his coach, upholstering the door, window-frames and seats with silk and velvet.*

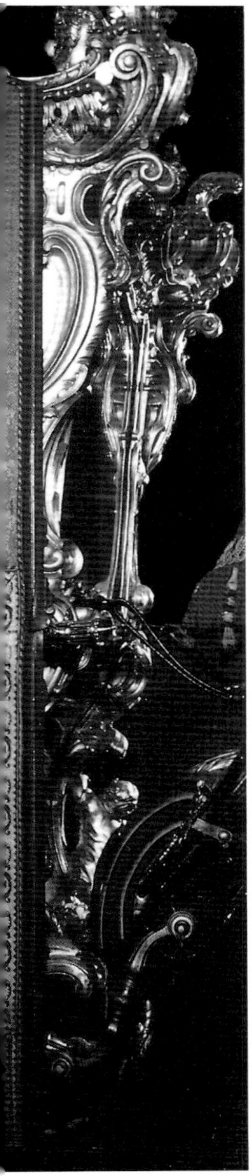

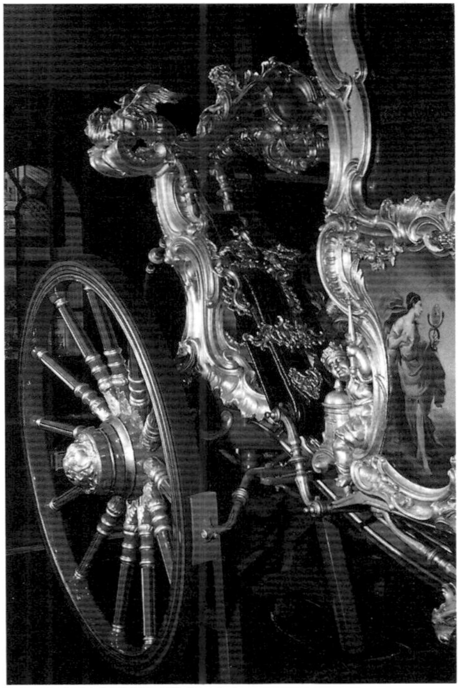

11 The back wheel brake is clearly visible, and also the leather braces attaching the Coach to the elaborately carved hindcarriage.

12 The harness worn by the team of drays supplied by Messrs Whitbread is also kept in the Museum.

Shoe-Maker; he finishes his Work by the Assistance of the Founder, Tire-Smith, Wheeler, Carver, and Painter: He is a Carpenter, as he frames the Body and Carriage of Wood; a Taylor, as he lines the Inside with Cloth, Silk, Velvet, or other Materials, to which he is obliged to use his Needle; and he is a Shoe-Maker, as he covers the Top and Sides with Leather, in which he is sometimes obliged to use his Awl.'

The coach-carver specialised exclusively in this branch of carving; the wheeler was employed in making the wooden part of the wheels; a class of founders who only worked for coach-makers cast the brasses of the body, the door-hinges, harness-buckles and all the other decorations made of brass or cast metal, while the tyre-smith made the ironwork including the springs but excluding the iron coach-buckles, which were delegated to yet another craftsman; finally, the coach-maker employed a tradesman to make the harness for the horses. Thus it was difficult for the maker to give the client an exact quotation, and according to a letter in the Corporation Records from Berry, on this occasion he sustained a loss.

The new Lord Mayor and Aldermen, however, must have been well pleased with their bargain. The coach was modern in design, being of the Berlin type, rather than the heavier *grand carrosse* design used for state coaches in the late seventeenth and early eighteenth centuries. Sir Robert Taylor is usually associated with the introduction of neo-Classicism to England, but from a series of designs he made for chimney-pieces, it appears he had a strong interest in the Rococo early in his career.

Rococo (first devised as a term of ridicule around 1800) approximates to the French *genre pittoresque*, brought to England in the 1730s by immigrant artists and craftsmen, or through pattern books and ornamental prints. By the 1740s, its influence was being felt in the applied arts produced by native carvers and engravers. Irregularity, asymmetry, elegance and lightness were the principal elements of the style.

13-16 Forecarriage of the Coach showing the coachman's scallop footrest and details: one of the two tritons supporting the coachman's seat (above left); the sheep's head under the seat; and one of the two sea-serpents heading the carriage.

17-19 Hindcarriage of the Coach (facing page, above); surmounted by a putti *with a fish tail supporting the City arms; and the swan nestling above a bearded mask at the base.*

Although closely dependent on French models, the Lord Mayor's Coach offers a robust interpretation of the genre in its exuberant style of carving. Happily, the Rococo penchant for *rocaille* – flowing patterns loosely derived from marine rocks and crustacea – can be seen as exemplifying London's pre-eminence as a port. The coach is attached by means of leather braces to an elaborately carved fore- and hindcarriage headed by sea serpents . The coachman's seat is supported by powerful tritons and his footrest is formed from a scallop shell. The hindcarriage is composed of a forcefully articulated cartouche, surmounted by *putti* (one with a fish tail) supporting the City's arms, with fire-breathing dragons at both edges. A swan nestles at the base, above a bearded mask. *Putti* representing the four continents support the coach at each corner: Asia and Africa in front with America and Europe behind them. Between the wheels under the coachman's seat, the mask of a sheep's head symbolises the foundation of London's wealth on the wool trade.

The paintings in the coach panels *(20-27)* feature the allegorical figure of the Genius of the City. In the upper panel at the rear, she is attended by Neptune and receives representatives of Trade and Commerce bearing goods from around the world: cornucopia of fruit, elephant tusks, an Arabian stallion and a lion; in the painting below, Riches and Plenty pour coins and fruit in her lap. On the right hand side, she is enthroned against a background of old St Paul's, and Fame bearing a laurel wreath presents to her a Lord Mayor; on the left, she stands with Mars who points with his spear to the scroll held by Truth on which is inscribed the name of Henry FitzAlwin, the first Mayor of London. The panel at the front of the coach depicts Faith beside a sacrificial altar supporting Charity, while Hope points to the dome of St Paul's. The side panels are decorated with female figures representing the Virtues: Truth, Temperance, Justice and Fortitude. The paintings are attributed to Giovanni Battista Cipriani (1727-85), who arrived in London from Rome in 1755 and is known to

20 To symbolise London's mercantile might, the Genius of the City is depicted receiving an exotic array of goods from round the world, including elephant tusks, an Arabian stallion and a lion.

21 Enthroned above old St Paul's, the Genius of the City receives a Lord Mayor who is escorted into her presence by Fame.

22 The Genius of the City confers with Mars, who points with his spear to a scroll, bearing the name of Henry FitzAlwin, the first Lord Mayor of London, who has been brought before them by Truth.

23 Detail of the front panel depicting Hope pointing to the dome of St Paul's.

24 (top left) The Virtue of Truth is depicted holding up her mirror; the crowned putti *beside her represents Europe, with a sceptre in one hand and a classical model Pantheon in the other. The designer, Sir Robert Taylor, was to incorporate a rotunda based on the Pantheon into the extensions he made to the Bank of England in the 1760s.*

25 (top right) The Virtue of Temperance holds a bridle, while the putti *representing Africa is attached to the Coach by a scorpion and clutches a Horn of Plenty in his left hand.*

26 (lower left) The Virtue of Justice is depicted blindfold with sword and scales; the putti *representing Asia is wreathed in flowers and opens a chained coffer of incense.*

27 (lower right) The Virtue of Fortitude stands beside her pillar in a stormy landscape; the putti *representing America is dressed as an Indian king, with a feathered head-dress, bow and quiver of arrows.*

have executed the paintings for Chambers' royal state coach. A drawing in one of his albums of designs is certainly related to the figure Justice on the Lord Mayor's Coach.

Before the technological innovations of the machine age, the distinction between the fine and applied arts was not strictly applicable. Cipriani painted both history paintings, the most elevated category in the hierarchy of art, and decorative schemes. Charles Catton (1728-98) trained as a coach-painter, and rose to become coach-painter to George III; he also studied at the St Martin's Lane Academy, and painted landscapes, animals and occasionally portraits and history. Like Cipriani in 1768 he became a Foundation member of the Royal Academy of Arts. The furniture-maker John Linnell (1723-96) attended the St Martin's Lane Academy and was a fluent draughtsman from both a design and technical point of view. He was responsible for the state coach of George, Prince of Wales in 1783, which was decorated by Robert Smirke (1752-1845), another Academician.

Such instances of artistic collaboration grew increasingly rare as the technology became more advanced and the maker was tempted to economise on the decoration. The Lord Mayor's Coach serves as both a splendid testimony to the successful alliance between architect, maker, carver and painter, and an annual reminder of an age when London was a city of unmatched wealth and pride.

SELECTED READING

Marcus Binney, 'Apotheosis of the Rococo: The Lord Mayor's Coach', *Country Life*, clxiv (1978), pp. 1596-8.

Marcus Binney, *Sir Robert Taylor: From Rococo to Neo-Classicism* (London, 1984).

Tessa Murdoch, 'The Lord Mayor's Procession of 1686: the Chariot of the Virgin Queen', *Transactions of the London and Middlesex Archaeological Society*, xxxiv (1983), pp. 207-12.

Robert Raines, 'Drawings by Marcellus Lauron – "Old Laroon" – in the Pepysian Library, *Apollo*, lxxxii (1965), suppl. pp. 2-4.

Sheila Williams, 'The Lord Mayor's Show in Tudor and Stuart Times', *Guildhall Miscellany 1*, no. 10 (1959), pp. 3-18.

Rococo Art and Design in Hogarth's England (Victoria and Albert Museum exhibition catalogue, 1984).

On Lord Mayor's Day each year, the carriage wheels are placed on a ramp, a cantilevered bridge raised and panels opened.

The Coach is wheeled out of the Museum into the open air at the west end of London Wall.

Messrs Whitbread's drays are harnessed to the Coach.

The Coach proceeds along London Wall to the Mansion House.